EPITOME OF PATIENCE

SHIPRA GUPTA

Made with ♥ on the Notion Press Platform
www.notionpress.com

To my adorable Grandfather Late Shri Sahaj Ram Gupta and to my Grandmother Smt. Basanti Devi and to my father Mr. Satyender Gupta

Special Thanks to my Mother Mrs. Rajulika Gupta and to my Husband CA Gaurav Agrawal for always motivating me to do something better.

Contents

A Letter To Grandpa — vii

1. The Day That Changed Everything — 1

2. Last Year — 8

3. Brother Sister Bond — 15

4. Career Conciousness — 20

5. Loving Moments With Grandmom — 24

6. Daily Routine — 28

7. Memorable Childhood — 33

8. School Days — 38

9. Silent Cry — 41

10. Last Day Out — 44

11. The Eschaton — 47

Epilogue — 53

A Letter To Grandpa

Dear Grandpa,

I miss you so much. It's just impossible for me to keep you out of my memories. I used to miss you on daily basis and not only me but Grandmom, father and rest everyone in our family keep missing you. On various occasions, we used to feel short without you.

Festivals don't have that much fun now. As you were senior in our home, every small worship and offerings to God started by you first but now we used to miss those moments. You are next to God for all of us. Worshipping the God or giving respect to you were the same things. You fulfilled our lives. In fact, I hate to use the past tense here for you because you went nowhere for me, you are still here for all of us.

Home is no home without you. At every step of my life, when I feel weak, I used to remember you and saw you in my dreams where you listen to my problems like before. You are inseparable part of my life. I can't imagine my life without your sweet memories. No one else could ever take your place in my life. I wish you could be with us and specially with our grandmom who used to miss you every single day. I know you always wanted to live more. Time deceives you otherwise everything was going well. I wish nature could give you some more time.

We used to keep your favourite things intact. Like we have kept your money plant growing and other plants are flourishing as well. We never bother grandmom also for any matter and try to keep her happier in your absence as now she is the only gem we have left with. We do take care of her at our best.

Wherever is your soul now, I wish it could rest in peace and keep us blessed as always. Love you to the moon and ahead Baba!

Your loving grand daughter

Shipra!

CHAPTER ONE

The day that changed everything

11 JULY 2018

The day when I was thinking about some kind of celebration at night because it's the wedding anniversary of my mom and dad. I was planning a little surprise for both of them with my siblings. Parents as the word itself filled with lots of emotions & feelings, right? We, the grown-up adults always wanted to do something for them. But do the parents mean only our father and mother. Well, maybe yeah in some cases they only consist of mom and dad but only for those who don't have the GRANDPARENTS.

Yup, Grandparents, the word that is filled even with a lot more feelings and emotions. Everyone is not lucky enough to have them all in their life. Here again I don't mean by grandparents only from father's side but from mom's side too.

Yeah, the truth is you really will consider yourself lucky if you have them from both sides. Well, I was the lucky one since always in matter of having a complete family. I have them all six as parents & others too.

From others I mean.... yeah, Annoying Siblings, your whole-time buddies, your crime partners in all the follies. When we are with our siblings, we literally hate them and when we live apart, we literally miss them too much.

We all love this kind of happy family. And somewhere we want that everything should be continued in the same way for whole life. We never want to miss the fun of family even if we'd achieve heights in our career or professional life.

It's not surprising to see that even a billionaire needs a happy family because money can't buy everything. One could feel his every penny earned worthless if we don't have a family to share happiness with.

In fact, most of the people do something astonishing in their life for sake of their family. They want them to give every kind of happiness of the world. World seems empty without a family of your own even if it is filled with lot others to whom you are familiar with, because those other familiar individuals can't replace the fun of being with family.

Still there are some poor ones who don't understand the importance of having a family at all. They only are the machines to earn that green piece of paper which at ends can't buy celestial happiness for us, only it could buy us some luxuries, the exhilaration of which is incomplete without our near and dear ones.

Simply it could be said that all these amenities are worthless without all of them without which we don't ever want to imagine our lives.

Even we could look at our Hollywood and Bollywood stuff. Around 90 cent stories revolve around family. The cultures they are depicting make us learn about family values. Family – this word itself linked to lot of sentiments. Like all others I do have a loving family too but time doesn't remain same forever.

<u>GRANDPA'S LIFE</u> -

So, it's the day time, I was baking a cake. All are at home except my father who's returning from the Meerut city with blood test & other reports of my grandfather. During his travel time he just opened the sealed reports and found something unusual related to tumours. Although not being from medical field it's quite hard to understand the exact problem.

Then he decided to text me the data of the reports. I was still cooking at that time. Eagerly waiting for the evening time, unaware of what's going to happen till evening.

This is what we all do. When we are planning for something, we sometimes so much loose ourselves in that stuff, we just forget what's going around and just start overlooking everything.

I have a friend of mine from medics still studying but having a good practical exposure. I usually send him the reports of the doctors of my family members to reach an instant rough conclusion of the actual scenario. I did the same thing once again. I send him the reports of my grandfather.

"Hey! Please interpret these reports, if there is something serious then tell me." I texted

Within next one minute my cell beeps and here was the reply-

"Whose reports are these?"

"Is there something serious", I asked eagerly.

"First tell me the name of person of whom are these reports in your family" he again replied.

"My grandfather"

"Oh!"

"Why? What happened?" I stopped cooking for a while & hold the phone tightly gazing it without blinking. I sensed something is wrong with the reports.

Somewhere I knew he won't give me the inaccurate conclusion because he has a lot more exposure in this field.

And then he said "He is not well"

"And what do you mean by it exactly?" (Eyebrows raised) I looked over the reports trying to get the meaning through googling. It's related some kind of tumour of which I was not sure what exactly it was.

"He has got Cancer and could survive only for next few days." He replied eventually.

A certain kind of silence captured me. Suddenly I reached to a thoughtless state. A state which you attained after practicing meditation for years i.e., a thoughtless state. I reached there suddenly. I was like unable to think. Suddenly a tear rolled down my eye. And here comes my mom in the kitchen asking what has happened to me. I was unable to reply. I want to forget everything like a dream.

Some times when we saw a bad dream, we want to forget it ASAP because it makes us uncomfortable thinking what will happen if this dream comes true. What we will do in that situation and blah blah blah...!! Many thoughts occupied our mind in the morning when we woke up after such dreams.

What we like to dream always a mythos life, full of joys & peace all around. From such kind of dreams, we just never want to wake up.

Then my phone rings and I got out of that other world. My friend was calling because I suddenly stopped replying him. He wants me to ask my wellbeing after hearing that news. I picked up the call, unable to say a single word.

"Where are other family members.", he asked

"All are here, except my father, he's on his way to home from hospital." I replied in shattered tone.

"You, okay??"

"Are you sure about the reports?" I asked thinking that something will change. Maybe he interpreted it in wrong way. Maybe he will say that I read someone else's reports.

"I know this moment is quite heavy for you. But give your grandfather a general treatment instead of chemotherapy because the process is quite painful and I afraid maybe he won't be able to cope up with same. But it's for sure he will feel unbearable and endless pain when his last time will come. So, it's time to try to keep him happier and more engaged in other activities."

I was unable to figure out what he was talking about. Maybe I was acting like deaf even after listening carefully because it's hard to accept the truth. Sighing a deep breath, I asked "How much time he has left now?"

"May be two or three months. Just take him to a good doctor nearby and start the normal treatment."

"Humm, I will!! Talk to u later my father is calling." I lied to end up our conversation. May be this is what we all do when we don't want to continue anymore over call.

Completely shattered I texted my father that grandpa had figured out with last stage cancer. My father loves his father a lot but he never expressed his feelings with anxiety same like my grandpa. My father used to remain calm. But I knew at this moment he shredded tears too. Although I was not seeing him live but I could sense his feelings.

Within few minutes my mom who was eagerly listening to my conversation understood the whole scenario. I started breathing heavily and cried hard for almost an hour. Then I rushed to my grandpa's room.

He was sitting as usual on his sofa, smiling, looking peaceful, unaware of the circumstances, doing his journal entries related to book keeping work which he used to do as part time job since I knew him. Aah, can't ever forget that reposeful face of him. I looked at him, he smiled towards me and started focusing over his work again without getting being disturbed by my presence, uninformed of what was going on inside his body.

I wanted that moment to be stopped forever. I never wanted to tell him anything or make him feel uncomfortable. Because who liked to hear such news that he or she has only got nearly two or three more months to live. Only a few are courageous enough to handle the same.

I knew my grandpa well. He is not afraid of getting died because he knew well that death is the only truth of the world. He is very spiritual but I knew one more thing that he wanted to live for some more time with all of us. He wanted to me get married in front of him. He wanted to see my sister getting a good job. He wanted to see his two other grandsons getting good grades in studies. But all in vain now.

I sat beside my grandpa seeing him working with teary eyes. It's hard to control my emotions before him. I just wanted to sit alongside of him forever & wanted to talk nonstop.

Suddenly everything gets paused. And I saw grandpa sitting in front of me & saying "I know why you are worried because you don't want to lose me. I also don't want to go but sometimes situations are not in our control. We just can't make them work in our own way. Sometimes we just have to let it go. You just need to understand sometimes, may be things worked in this way only, predestined, that's all I could say!"

"I can't imagine my life without you grandpa. I have lived my whole life with you. I never learned to live without you. Sometimes I prayed to God that if you want to cut down my age then you may cut but give a healthy life to my grandparents"

And suddenly I came out of hallucination. Again, in the same reality, this time grandpa looking at me in an amusing way & asked what happened to me, and I replied trying to give a fake smile "Nothing"

Then we along with my grand mom had some evening snacks with some good laughs. I really never enjoyed this togetherness this much as I was enjoying on that particular day.

<u>WHAT I LEARNED</u>-

When we have all the time to enjoy something we rarely enjoy those things, because somewhere we think that it's our daily routine life and we could recreate these moments all over again whenever we want. But trust me, we never realise that every moment is for limited duration and precious until it's gone. Once the moment has gone, we can't rejoice that particular moment again.

We can't hold any moment. We have no power to hold. So, it's always better to live each and every moment to the fullest when we are confronting the same.

As we grow older, we forget that our parents are also getting older and we got so much busy in our lives, we almost forget that they also need our time, care & some moments together only.

It's the simple rule of the nature that what we give out, comes back to us in unusual ways. If we give time and respect to our parents, only then we could expect the same from our future generation. We are moving with the wheel of time. One day we also get old and at that time money can't bought happiness to us but our family does. Money is just source of living not the means of happiness. Family is the only mean of happiness. We need to accept this very fact eventually.

And in that evening, we haven't celebrated the anniversary of my parents. I just spend the whole evening cherishing old memories with my grandparents listening to their stories which I had almost listen like a thousand times before because that time I didn't know which day would be grandpa's last. In case of diseases like cancer we can't hope for the best because there is still no permanent cure for cancer. Hospice care can keep you free of pain and other symptoms of painful cancer treatments.

CHAPTER TWO

LAST YEAR

Last year than explained in previous chapter bought our family another tragic incident. It was like life doesn't want to manifest in, for my grandpa. Somehow, he survived that incident last year but life had other surprises for him in very next year.

Previous year in the mid of June, another incident took place in my grandpa's life. But at that time, I had the faith that I will make everything good in his life once again. There are times in everyone's life which are painful but somewhere we know that hard time will pass gradually and the season of blossom will bloom again. Like in the times of COVID 19 outbreak, whole world was facing lockdown, deaths and distress all where but we all had the faith that it won't last forever. Time will change as Change is the only constant and inevitable.

But when the hard time comes, we usually lost our wisdom & become distressed. We are not ready to understand the difference between right or wrong at that time. Sometimes this continuous situation could lead us to depression as only the depressing thoughts start to come inside our brain. Our brain needs some kind of conditioning at that time, some good thoughts to replace the negative ones.

It's nearly impossible to stay positive all the time. It feels good to read the good books to stay positive & think only positive thoughts but living this kind of life in real is completely different. It's pragmatic to deal with things sensibly and realistically in a way that is based on practical rather than theoretical considerations. We need to learn it throughout the life through different experiences. I also learned the same steadily.

<u>GRANDPA'S LIFE -</u>

My grandpa used to go on evening walk on daily basis. There he used to meet his friends of same age group & converse for long hours. In childhood we as kids used to wander with grandpa in the parks. Grandpa used to hold our little hands to the park & let us play there for almost an hour. I really enjoyed those walks a lot. On the way to the park, he used to teach me various things by giving practical knowledge like the process of plantation, water cycle process, various reasons of different pollutions, history of trains as we could also see running trains on the track from the park, how to become a locomotive engineer, reasons to admire the nature and a lot more stuff.

Slowly with the passage of time we become adults and got busy with our lives. Now, sometimes I raised question to myself that why we forget to recreate those little fun moments again which we used to cherish in our childhood even we have the chance to live those moments again. I don't remember after becoming so called adult when was the last time I went on an evening walk with my grandpa. I didn't but I should go at least once a week because you never know how much time you have left with that particular person.

Grandpa becomes older with passage of time and evening walks started making him feel more exhausted. I used to orate him to not to go outside anymore because of his age and heavy traffic but he never breaks his daily routine. He used to bring us fruits on the way to home in evening. One very day he was coming from his routine walk and with fruits in hands then suddenly a monkey attacked him for want of fruits. It was so sudden surprise for my grandpa that he lost his balance and fell down over the street just a few steps from home. Soon the public gathered to help the old man lying there and one acquaintance of him somehow managed to take him to home. He was not injured on the outer side but got internal injury not visible at first.

But the friend of my grandpa who brings him home repeatedly requested me to call for an ambulance for X-Ray purpose. I contemplate the situation then call a cab to the hospital and got an X-ray report. In report we found that his hip bone of the right side got fractured and he was in enormous pain. Only thing that amazed me that he still was in peaceful mode bearing all the pain without groaning. What kind of person he was, I never understood. How could someone be so calm in such life-threatening situation just not to bother the family members, he kept quiet and waited so long to get rid of the pain itself.

Doctors admitted him in the hospital that night. That was for the first time since my birth, I saw my grandpa in the hospital. He had never seen the face of the hospital as he didn't have any kind of diseases like Sugar, high cholesterol, blood pressure related issues and even any hearing or vision related problems. Because of healthy living style, my grandpa was perfectly fine even in the oldest age. He was so much disciplined since always, any health-related issue can't touch him ever. I wish I could be more like him. He has so many qualities to learn from.

Alas, that night my father stayed in the hospital with him and I came back to home disheartened. We then delivered this news to our grandmom who didn't have dinner that always saw my grandparents having all the meals of the day together only starting from morning tea. That night was very hard for all of us.

With slow pace time has passed and the very next morning doctors suggested for the operation of hip bone with eighty cent rates of success. Doctors generally insert a kind of rod to support the hip for hip surgery. Most people are able to return to work four weeks to four months after surgery. But it may take six months to one year for you to fully recover. Some people, especially older people, are never able to move quite as well as they used to. You heal best only when you take good care of yourself. But surgery in older age is very risky because of various infection related reasons. You need complete bed rest.

Doctors gave us two options either to take away patient home and leave him on his condition with pain killers for rest of his life or to take the risk of the surgery. Being uncomfortable with the first one we decided to choose the other one and booked a surgery to one of the best surgeons nearby for my grandpa following two days after the incident took place. After the surgery my grandpa came home with a whole list of prescriptions from the doctor's side. He was not even allowed to move from a certain position because of the stitches. Seeing him like this in this age was the hardest thing to do for all of us.

Only thing now could recover him the good care. I talked to my grandpa after his return to home. He has tears in his eyes. That was the most painful moment for him to see my him in this miserable state. But I could do nothing to cure him instantly. He had lost all his willpower to recover and to live again like before because now he was not able to walk like before. Now he can't work like before, not even able to sit like before. Everything has changed for him. Now he has to live in a different reality and it's hard to accept this reality at first for an active person like him.

He uttered, "My life has now come to an end. I won't survive for more days now. I can't bear this pain anymore now."

I replied, "Nothing to worry about grandpa. I will take care of you in every possible manner. I won't leave you alone."

He ordered, "No, you can leave. I don't need anyone. I know I won't survive now."

I said, "You have to live for all of us. I wanted to get married one day in your presence only with your blessings. You're not allowed to go anywhere."

Grandpa sighed, "You are not understanding what I'm going through. I can't even move myself."

"It's just a matter of time grandpa. I know you are in immense pain but you have to rise again for sake of all of us, especially for our grandmom. She is also not eating properly seeing you like this."

"But I'm helpless now. I also want to live for one more year. I also prayed to God during my surgery to give me one more year to live so that I could see you getting married before Me.", he replied ambitiously.

"God can't be this much cruel to you. He will listen to you for sure. Just try for one last time for all of us." I requested.

Even after convincing by all of us, he repeatedly denied taking care of him, even having the daily meals for almost a week. He also got bed sores. Then we have to admit him again in the hospital for few days seeing his worsening condition. Everything was falling apart in my life. I was unable to find a way back to grandpa. After healing from bedsores, he came back to home again.

He has lost all his will power to fight with this tough time. As far as I knew him, he was the one who didn't give up quite easily. He is the man to fight till end and to rise once again on being fallen in any scenario. He is ideal person for everyone. It's difficult to find someone like him in today's scenario. He had finest control over him. I never saw him being in angry state. I always saw him in a smiling face and chanting 'Hare Rama, Hare Krishna, Krishna Krishna, Hare Hare'. He used to read ancient scriptures to learn something meaningful and also made it read to me sometimes whenever I visited him in the whole day.

But now seeing him losing all the consciousness and becoming stubborn just because of physical pain, I got saddened. I decided not to leave him alone for whole day. I took leaves from my job and started taking care of him. From his daily dressing of wounds to food and medicines, I took charge of every petty issue in my hands leaving all other members to rest mode. I used to clean his room by myself daily and sanitize everything properly. I changed his bed sheets on daily basis and started washing his clothes all by myself. I also started doing grandpa's part time accounting work with my sister's help. I took care of his plants and used to water them daily. I used to read to him old scriptures of his choice. In short, I started taking care of every little aspect related to him. Seeing all of us so much enthusiastic and positive my grandpa again started to gain lost confidence. Within a month he again started to have daily meals properly. We used to create a healthy environment around him and crack jokes often to change his mood. My grandmom relieved after seeing improvement in his mental health.

Then we appointed a physiotherapist for grandpa's exercise so that he could walk all over again like before. In starting he denied to have physiotherapy but with the support of therapist he started doing a little exercise on daily basis. After it he started having his food by his own hands and started to sit slowly all by himself without our support.

Within fifteen days, therapist made him stand and walk with the help of walker. My grandpa also has the strong willpower to walk again like before. So, he learned quite quickly to walk without our support. And within next fifteen days, he started walking with the help of wooden walking stick leaving the walker behind.

"That's like my brave grandpa." I screamed with joy that day.

<u>WHAT I LEARNED-</u>

This is what happened with us at some stage in our lives. When we get into any kind of trouble, we lose all our consciousness. We thought now we have to live in distress for lifetime but this isn't true. Time always has surprises for all of us. It changes very quickly. Tough times don't last forever. It's the unquestionable law of nature. Nature flourishes itself with life again after extinction. So, whenever you engaged in any difficulty observe it with PATIENCE and try to analyse the situation thoughtfully, then you will find yourself with solutions all around. As I heard a proverb, "Every problem comes with a solution. Only we have to find that solution."

Introspect yourself for few minutes a day on daily basis and miracles can happen in your life. It's all about taking a pause and looking where we are heading towards or where this road will lead us. We have to question ourselves on daily basis to find answers and for this we need a questioning mind. We are the pioneer of our life and it's always in our hands to change the direction of sail to achieve our planned targets. As Sandeep Maheshwari said, "No person is too small or too big, if you want to achieve some goal and if there is any single person who have achieved it, then you can achieve it too light-heartedly." Whether it's related to your career or your studies or your relationships or your family, only we need a strong willpower and fire in our belly to achieve the same.

CHAPTER THREE

BROTHER SISTER BOND

"She is wearing my top. Make her change the same, Mom!!", I screamed out of anger.

"She also wore my jeans, previous month and that too without my permission." My sister replied in the same scale of tone.

"Shut up you both morons." My mom wailed.

I used to fight a lot with my younger sis in my childhood. She is the only sibling I do have. We didn't even realize we were making memories; we just knew we were having fun. This saying by Winnie the Poohnow started making sense to me. We generally spend our childhood fighting with our siblings or making them feel irritated with our stupid acts. All these moments make us feel good after getting separated in youth due to career or wedding or due to any other cause. The bond of sisters and brothers is so strong that maybe they can't live with each other but definitely they also can't live without.

We should value relationships when we are having, we-time together because time once gone never going to come back again. You can't recreate same moments again. These moments can't even be bought with money. Only the development of understanding is needed to cherish each and every moment in life so that you can enjoy the life to the fullest.

<u>GRANDPA'S LIFE -</u>

In the life story of my grandpa, he had born after three sisters of him i.e., he was the younger one. He lived in a joint family. At the very early age of five, my grandpa loses his both parents and rest all of his sisters got married one by one. After wedding of his last elder sister my grandpa becomes so much lonely. His uncles didn't take care of him like his own kids. He started to feel unwanted and alone in that very early age. If something bad happens to us at early childhood, impact of that is long term. A childhood with all the facilities and parents love is truly a blessing.

One day, his sister visited to meet his only brother. There she saw he was crying for a toy since long and no one was there to give attention to him. His elder sister loved his younger brother so much, she took him to her husband's family and take care of him like a mother then. She also gave him good education so that he would become capable of living on his own. My grandpa was a brilliant student since always. He got A plus grades and cleared government job exams & finally chosen to serve Central Railways. That is how he got settled in his life after so many struggles.

My grandpa's sister was his mother, his father, his mentor, his everything. Their bond is just unbreakable and irreplaceable. No one else could take place of his sister in his life ever. He just loves her so much. I remember in front of me also grandpa used to visit his sister every month and she used to visit our home too on a regular basis. My grand mom also had a nice bonding with her.

Gradually with passing of time his sister becomes older & more prone to diseases. She got on bed for almost two months before her passing away. I still remember her last day because that was the hardest day for my grandpa. On her last day my grandpa visited her. He was visiting after every two or three days to see her as she was on bed completely dependent on a nurse. My grandpa told they both hold hands of each other and had a deep eye connection. Her pale eyes still recognize her dear younger brother. They both had nothing to say. Only the tears of separation could be seen.

That day Grandpa returned to home with heavy heart and sat on sofa and the very next moment he received a call that his dearest sister has left the world. He broke down completely on that day and I saw him crying for the very first time in my life. His world just felt apart that day. The pain of separation only could be felt by that person who undergoes that pain, for others it is just an intimation of death. He tried to hide his pain, still can't resist the flow. I was very younger to feel grandpa's feelings at that time. My whole family consoled him specially my grand mom because she knew well what my grandpa has just lost. The bonding of my grandparents was more than true love and can't be expressed in words. They understood well each other like no one else could ever.

Slowly with passage of time, grandpa's pain healed. Time is the best healer. Time flies but memories last forever in our heart. We just somehow learn to live without those persons without whom we think it's impossible to live life. I like the nature of kids under ten in this matter because they are the only individuals who know well how to maintain the balance of emotions. Neither they mourn for death nor do they rejoice the birth. Youth tries to learn this technique through meditation but kids have inbuilt quality which lapses with time generally.

WHAT I LEARNED-

Sometimes I compare my own life with grandpa and get to know how much easy my life was since birth. I always got needed attention as well as feeling of security from my parents as well as grandparents too. I never get worried for who will pay for my education and other bills. Generally, we all are blessed with so many blessings, that we forget to count the same & to express gratitude for. We need to start counting on our blessings. Make a list and you will notice many such things which you didn't notice before.

We can see, hear, speak, taste, touch & feel. It's a real bliss. Think for a moment and compare yourself with a person having disability like of not seeing or listening or speaking, you will find yourself in a much better place. Having healthy physique is also a blessing. If you compare yourself with a person who is a patient of malnutrition or suffering from any other no curable disease then you will realize for sure that health is a true wealth indeed and seriously you will find many people around, not capable of enjoying good health.

Having a family of your own with parents, siblings, grandparents and others is also a blessing. In today's scenario, there is new concept emerging of nuclear family. Most people around are getting separated or don't want to live in a joint family due to various reasons. Living separate is not a problem; the real issue is dying feelings or emotions inside. Now a days we have got so much busy with our lives so we forget to spend time with our parents or other near & dear ones and even we don't have the time to make a call to them. Only the social media- What's app, Instagram or Facebook becomes the media to connect.

All these lead to increase in nonverbal communication in place of verbal one. Verbal communication is also a need to evolve hidden emotions in youth. The more you talk, the more you reflect your emotions, stronger your relation becomes with your loved ones.

Having good degrees or career or communication skills or having a fully functional mind with many other capabilities or talents, all are real blessings from mother nature. It's necessary to cherish your blessings otherwise it's just only you are living with a family but not LIVING moments in reality.

We must be thankful to our parents who not only gave us this beautiful life but also makes it purposeful. They are our lifesavers, security givers, educator, love giver, caretaker and just everything. It's not the duty of parents to provide us everything just because they give us birth but they do everything out of love, still we can't realize the same until we become parents. It's impossible to see life from the perspective of parents until we get into the same position.

We must give adequate respect to parents because raising a kid to an adult is not an easy task to do. You have to invest a considerable part of your life to cultivate another life. It's our duty to give at least one tenth part of our lives to our parents who gave us their almost one third part of life. Children are the biggest investments of parents, so be their highest paid returns. They don't need you financially because if they could raise you to earn that green paper of currency, they could raise themselves too even in their old age. They just need your emotional support and mental assistance to live happily after retirement from their parental job.

The same concept applies on siblings too. We just need to be present mentally for them too because after parents they are the only ones who are our true mates. Let's not get busy into our lives so much so that we forget that we have other's also whom we are losing somewhere amidst the battle to earn bread. Because when we got old, we no longer needed money to be contended but always want our near and dear ones to share our past memories with, to laugh together. After all life is short, get the best out of it. You may never know which day could be your last. So, live each day like it's your last. Make that phone call today which you put on hold thinking when he or she doesn't want to call me then why should I call first. Take the initiative, call your near and dears and say just wanted to know your wellbeing and see the magic of relations. They will flourish with a deep and unbreakable bond.

CHAPTER FOUR

CAREER CONCIOUSNESS

There are two major decisions in a person's life in general; first one is Career and another one is Marriage. These are the concerns on which a person's whole life depends. It took almost one third of our life to settle down with both above decisions. Next one third generally spend on raising children and last one third in cherishing what we have done so far.

In today's time we need an early retirement to really enjoy life by exploring various countries or doing things which we haven't done earlier due to lack of time or other reasons. For this purpose, we need a good career for which consciousness is needed at very early age. Children with conscious parents achieve success earlier than those whose parents aren't so much active. Successful parents can educate their children in a better way and make them proactive since birth because they know the value of education so they always help their kids in increasing their talents.

<u>**GRANDPA'S LIFE -**</u>

In the life story of my grandpa, he was the one who knows the value of education. Being from a rural area and raised without parents only with the help of his elder sister, he knew well the only thing that could make him successful in life was gaining more & more knowledge through studies. So did the same, he gained excellent knowledge of commerce and along with his government job he started part time accounting work of various entities to run his own family smoothly.

Grandpa does have six daughters and two sons as there was no awareness of family planning in

1950's. He has to bear the responsibilities of all. Along with fulfilment of basic necessities, he also invested in good education for all. He knew well only an educated person could get respect in society. For my father, he invested one third of his limited earnings per month to pay for the dues of the school. My father got education in the reputed school of that time which could only be afforded by affluent persons of that time. Only ten students in one standard got chance to study in that school and my father is one among them. It's all because of efforts of my grandpa who never gave up even in tough times.

With the efforts of my grandpa, my father also cracked government job exams and got chance to serve central railways. I used to admire my grandpa in this matter because first he gave good education to all and then get all his kids married and then build his own house with his savings. All this he has done with one job and part time accounting work.

In my case, my mom is a teacher. She has developed a keen interest of mine in studies since 1st standard. I used to study a lot with the help of my mom. She has invested a considerable time of her life in teaching me and my sister along with her private school job & household chores responsibilities which always seems a tough task to do. I also had a daily routine of learning English language from my grandpa. He had very good handwriting as well as good knowledge of English. He helped me in understanding basics of grammar since very early age. He used to read me stories of Shakespeare like Hamlet, Macbeth, King Lear etc. I used to enjoy learning from my grandpa on daily routine basis.

My grandpa always encouraged me to do something big in my life. He always inspired me with his daily routine as I have never seen any laziness inside him ever. He was the most active person I have ever known since always. I always saw him working and managing things in a way which should be followed by all of us. My grandparents lived their lives in the most disciplined way. I always had something to learn from their daily routine life. They both also used to recite me various epics of our Hindu mythology. There was always something to learn from those religious literatures.

With the efforts of my mom, I and my younger sister used to achieve first positions in our class since 1st standard and it made our grandparents to feel proud of us always. They used to share this happiness in the whole neighbourhood and also to the relatives. To see them this much happy made me to perform even better than before. I remember whenever I didn't focus on studies my grandpa used to say,

"Read it again carefully & slowly. First develop your understanding about the topic only then you could be able memorise it forever."

He used to repeat these lines again and again until it became part of my habit to understand first and memorise later on. Grandpa used to say we should never give up in any tough situation. By trying again and again we could get the desired success eventually. Only the firm determination is needed. He also advised me to be in good company of friends where you could learn one additional thing which you never knew before.

<u>WHAT I LEARNED-</u>

There is always something to acquire from other persons only if you know what to learn and how to apply in your own life. Learning is something which is a lifelong process. Career consciousness is not all about having a successful career with a reputed job; it's also about grooming your personality in a pragmatic way. Personality development generally depends on your level of education. The higher would be your knowledge level, the more you could groom yourself as a person. You will always find yourself at a different platform with the power of knowledge. Knowledge gives you more power and an appreciable level in the society. All respects a person having more knowledge than them. Knowledge enlightened us to live more happily in this materialistic world in a peaceful manner.

In general people have two options; either to start a good job or to start a good business for which you need a start-up idea but both are useless if you don't further enhance your knowledge. Most of the people in job are under pressure to maintain their current level earnings while there are some who used to get promotion every year from their current level. The only thing makes these people getting more success in short time is enhancement of knowledge at regular intervals. They didn't settle down to be at same place for their whole life.

Same is the case of the people doing business. To further expand their business, they need new innovative ideas and adaptability to change with latest prevailing circumstances. It could be done easily by gaining more and more knowledge of their current business. In business we generally use a term; SWOT Analysis. We need to do this analysis for us in our day-to-day life too.

S- Strength
W- Weakness
O- Opportunity
T- Threat

By this analysis we may come to know what we could have done the best and what should be least expected from us. We may also come to examine when the right time to grab the opportunity and what could be the possible barriers. It is just like doing introspection which helps one in reaching to their goals.

After all this, comes the satisfaction level. You need to decide where to stop running behind these materialistic things otherwise they will keep you running till end. By stopping you may see what you are leaving behind in this never-ending race of hunger. Life is too short so we forget to make all these decisions at early age still we need to decide it soon for ourselves so that we could spend the rest of our lives peacefully with our loving family creating moments of joy which amounts to everlasting happiness.

At the end when we look back at our lives, there should be no regrets of not doing those things which we always wanted to do or of not spending time with those with whom we always want to spend the same.

CHAPTER FIVE

LOVING MOMENTS WITH GRANDMOM

Togetherness is a word which itself contains a lot of emotions. When we are together with our loved ones, we often forget all our troubles and life seems to be at peace. We all love to be with our loved ones always viz our spouse, our parents or our siblings. The shit happens when we fell apart, that pain and suffering broke us down. It's our biggest nightmare to get separated from those around whom our day-to-day life revolves.

The human nature is to ensure its safety & security first, to live freely. In childhood we used to fear to lose our parents because we feel secure with them. In youth after getting married we used to fear to lose our partner because we can't imagine our life without them and then after having kids, we live in fear of ensuring their safety as well. In our whole life we always want our near and dear ones to stay interact with us. But all are not blessed enough to get togetherness with all near & dears in their lifetime. Some loses their parents at an early age; some loses their spouse and other near & dears due to whatever cause whether due to illness or accidental death or any other cause.

The thing that matters is how we treat others when we are with them. It's true that we all have to retire from this world one day but the impact we leave behind while living becomes the reason for others to keep us alive in their memories always. Only one percent of population of whole world does something remarkable and become able to mark their presence in the world history. Rest others are living their lives without any purpose. Even if we all are not capable of making history but we all at least could have a chance to create a room in the memories of our near and dear ones. We just need to show loving and caring attitude towards those who care for us & love us unconditionally.

<u>GRANDPA'S LIFE</u> -

The relation of my grandparents was very special. I haven't seen such couple in my entire life after them. The way they both care for each other and love each other made them inseparable like anything. I used to give their example to my friends. They got married at a very early age. My grand mom was just fifteen years old and grandpa was twenty-one and they got married in 1950's after independence of India. Both were together since that long time. As my grandpa has no parents so after marriage, they both used to live alone and manage things together.

With passage of time, they got kids, get them married and have grandchildren and just like any other ordinary story their sweet & loving story goes on. I have always seen them together since my childhood. I never saw them fighting or arguing like other couples. My grandpa had very peaceful nature and he never spoke a loud word to my grand mom. Such nature is rare to find in today's scenario as we used to argue even on petty issues with our loved ones. We place the issue on priority and relations on posteriority.

We need to understand that no issue is bigger than relations. We should focus on relations rather than useless issues because we can't take back the words once spoken. Choose your words wisely as they leave long lasting impact on the mind of one who listens. Still if someone said something in anger that could be ignorable, we should try to ignore and give importance to the person. A very few people are being capable of developing this quality. Only the people with deepest understanding level could develop it well.

My grandpa was one of them. He never argues over petty issues. He used to remain calm in every situation. He never spoke any word without thinking about it first. He was a good listener, first he listens carefully then analyse the situation and if necessary, then only reply. I never saw him engaged in any useless conversation with anyone. He used to do his accounting work on daily basis and read scriptures and various epics to gain more spiritual understanding. He knew well how to maintain inner peace. He rose over all the conflicts of materialistic world.

They used to celebrate all the festivals with fun and pleasure. On the occasion of 'Karva Chauth' my grandmom always keeps on fasting for grandpa and he also didn't have dinner without her. They both always wait for appearance of moon together and then open their fast. On other usual days also, they both always have their dinner together only. I just love to see both of them having so much in love.

I used to spend my evenings together with both of them. My grandpa used to crack old jokes and I laughed with him every time even if I were listening the same for 100th time. I also love to listen their old stories all over again because in that age everyone wants someone to listen to them. They neither need any materialistic thing nor any other luxuries, they just need your time and comfort zone.

I remember one very day in month of April 2017, I heard my grandparents were discussing about their wedding day. Then I joined the discussion and came to know that was their wedding day. For the first time I realised I never bothered to ask when they got married. That day I decided to celebrate their 65th anniversary. I started the preparations along with my siblings, ordered an eggless cake, decorated the room with balloons and invited relatives. Nothing needed that day to measure happiness of my grandparents; the emotions and happy reaction on their faces said it all. In evening we celebrated their special day and listened to their whole life journey with all the ears.

Now I can only cherish the pictures of that day because grandpa is no more now. My grand mom becomes lonely without him. They both lived together for more than 66 years and that amounts to a considerable part of someone's life. Even thought of separation after such a long time of togetherness makes me feel uncomfortable. My grand mom still follows their same daily routine even after demise of my grandpa. She still used to prepare evening tea for him & put it in front of grandpa's picture frame. Seeing her daily like this load me with lot of emotions. I hate the fact of separation of my grandparents. I love to see both of them together always.

<u>**WHAT I LEARNED-**</u>

Marriage is significant aspect of life, if mutual understanding exists otherwise, it's like spending life with a known with whom you have kids and you both have to live together for their sake and to maintain an image in society. Most of the marriages in our country go on, on the same pattern. Usually love stop existing between couples and they forget to enjoy togetherness while being together. When life comes to an end then the sudden realisation of not enjoying the same won't matters. It changes into regret all of a sudden. Life is all about creating moments when you are together with your loved ones i.e., Life exists in NOW. If you want to share some of your thoughts with your partner then do share the same without having any second thought. Do admire them or do tell 'em their mistakes. Maybe they'll improve or maybe they won't but just say it to reduce the burden of your thoughts to feel lighter. Life will pass in a blink and you even won't realise how far you have come.

I have seen my grandparents enjoying each and every moment while being together. They are like perfect example for me to follow. Life is too short so create moments; go on for a long-awaited vacation, do adventures which you have never done before, learn new things, develop new interests, never settle down in terms of enjoying life and invest your most of the time in grooming yourself. Life never gives us another chance. A moment once gone is gone forever and you can't buy it back even with your all monies.

CHAPTER SIX

DAILY ROUTINE

The daily routine of a person defines one's personality in certain manner. There should be discipline in our day-to-day routine at least in some aspects of life. As we should wake up early in the morning so that we could have time to plan our whole day. A day started in a pre-planned manner always gives fruitful results at the end. We should spare some time for routine exercise or morning walk, if not possible then for evening walk or a little workout. We must do these changes in our daily routine which is going to give no quick result in starting but a small positive change a day could be rewarding in long run.

Change could be of any kind, a positive change definitely going to affect you both physically and mentally. You will find yourself more active and closer to your goals otherwise an aimless life is worthless. When we start learning something new, in starting we need to push ourselves a bit hard. Slowly it will become part of our habit and healthy habits are always high yielding. We could start small with 5 minutes a day and linearly increasing the required time to pursue our interests. In this way our lives could become more fulfilling and we could become a better individual than we were before that start up.

Animals also have a routine life but they can't add up anything new to their daily routine due to restriction of having limited brain power but we humans are born with astonishing abilities and incredible brain power. If used in a positive way, we could provide meaning to our lives. Otherwise, one could regret for not having this or that or for not getting desired results in life. So, start small and make big changes with consistent efforts.

<u>GRANDPA'S LIFE -</u>

I used to notice all activities of my grandparents since birth. I wish I could be like them but I learned a lot of things from them during their lifetime. After all learning from others is important. They both had shared very special bond, giving couple goals to all. As part of their daily routine, both used to wake up at 4 A.M. in the morning daily and then clean their rooms and prayer room. Then they both read scriptures which look more like meditation to me. I used to join them in their morning prayers whenever possible. Then they both had their meals together, cooked by themselves only. They were so much independent for their own chores even in their old age; I just can't imagine myself doing the same in that age.

Routine work kept both of them engaged for whole day and it was the secret of their physical fitness even in their 80's. They both were so much fit, neither had they any medical problem related to physique like sugar or blood pressure or heart diseases which is very common in that age nor they had any mental issues related to loss of memory etc. And the only reason was their constant working attitude. They both used to say that Work is worship and they meant it too.

Grandpa used to read newspaper in morning. He used to mark various kind of educational news for me rather than focusing on unnecessary ones, he taught me to extract useful news from the newspaper. It helped me in enhancing my general knowledge of the world around me. I was very close to my grandparents since always. I keenly noticed them since always, so their every little act imprinted in my memory like forever.

My grandpa used to keep all his documents in a much systematic way. He has made files for every kind of documents like expenses file, savings file, bills file etc. In this way it becomes very easy to keep track on every petty issues. From this I have learned how to manage home issues effectively. Home management is an art and not all are expert in the same. Only a few with a clear vision could manage things well, even if we asked our grandpa for a 20 years old expense bill, he was able to find it in 20 seconds only due to fine management skills.

He used to teach me these skills as well, by showing me his work. Grandpa not only kept himself engaged in these routine tasks but he also knew how to enjoy life. I remember, he used to collect newspaper cutting of jokes corner and used to read it before all of us in the evening to have a good family time.

He also loved to watch cricket matches. He used to cheer up on seeing sixes of MS Dhoni, Yuvraj, Sehwag and other famous cricketers. Since he belongs to 90's, he was great fan of Kapil Dev and Sachin Tendulkar. In the absence of T.V., he used to listen commentary on his small pocket radio which he used to keep with himself. He also had routine to listen evening news over his pocket radio.

My grandpa also loved to do gardening. He had a small vacant piece of land where he used to grow different type of vegetables, fruits and flowers. He loved to take care of his plants even at home. He used to water them daily & protect them through transparent sheets during summer season to protect them from excessive heat. He took care of plants like a mother do of her child. I used to get inspired by him.

My Grandpa used to walk a lot. Grandpa's evening walk routine is fixed and unshakable. In childhood I used to go in walk with him. Grandpa used to admire nature and show me different shades of nature daily in the form of flowers, various trees, chirping birds, butterflies etc. Ah! Those days were so much calming and tranquil.

I remember he never took any public transport or any auto or rickshaw even for five-kilometre journey. He used to go on foot up to bank which was five kilometres away from home. He said walking kept him physically fit. But we all family members used to scare of this habit of grandpa because he was in his 80's now and walking up to that much distance seemed very hard to all of us because we are so much used to of using scooters or car even for such short distance. That's why maximum living age becomes less now.

Now a day's average maximum age of living is around sixty years while it was around eighty years for last generations. It's because mental work load has increased now and physical activities has decreased as well as happy time with family has decreased too.

People in the past used to live a tension free life because they have no demand of material amenities but now days, we have become more materialistic and want more comfort. In this world of artificial intelligence, we only want to move our fingers or our tongue to get the desired work done through different gadgets. We have become gadgets centred now. We don't even want to think what cost we are paying to have all this comfort. This comfort is making us lazier slowly. We need to step out of this comfort zone and have some physical activities back in life like we used to do in our childhood by playing different games. We need to get back that joyous childhood back in our lives, so that we could enjoy life for longer and could be at more peace.

Not only physical work routine but they also followed healthy diet routine. Healthy eating habits kept them free of various common diseases like fever, cold etc. I had never seen them using cold water directly from fridge, they always prefer to use earth pitcher to drink water or normal water. They used to do heavy breakfast but in afternoon only had 'Khichdi' or 'Dalia' as part of their daily routine to keep the balance interact. Fruits and green salad were part of their daily diet schedule in evening. They both used to have dinner up to 7 PM in the evening, so that they could have milk at night and go to bed by 9 PM. They used to keep dry fruits with them or other healthy eatables as part of snacks.

The above simple sober routine kept them in healthy condition. Only a healthy physique could have a healthy mind. A person which is fully contended by himself in terms of health only could place attention to other meaningful aspects of life. My grandpa knew it well. He taught me the true meaning of saying 'Health is Wealth'.

WHAT I LEARNED-

Mahatma Gandhi once said "Be the change you want to see in others". So did my grandpa taught me. First, he followed the routine then motivated me to follow the same too. Although it is impossible for me to follow it completely still, I always try my best to adopt some of grandpa's habits like I used to wake up by 6 AM and go to bed up to 10 PM. I used to have my dinner before 8 PM and always try to include healthy eatables like fruits and green vegetables in my daily diet.

It's impossible to have discipline in every aspect of life but we can start small by having discipline in few routine tasks. Many people have the courage to start a particular routine like gymming, yoga etc. but only a few have the desire to accomplish till end. For the purpose of accomplishment till end, first we need to understand our basic requirements to start anything and that should be clearly set as a goal in our mind, only then we could carry the same in long run.

Discipline can't be taught by someone through books or lectures, only one can motivate others to do better. It could be developed from inspiration within by practicing self-control over the time. My Grandpa was very much attached with plants and the same attachment I could feel in myself with my gardening hobby. I also take care of plants like a child and love to grow different veggies as well. I also love to paint them with acrylic colours with warli art and different patterns. Elders plays a great role in our life in developing our interests. We can learn many things if we closely follow them.

CHAPTER SEVEN

MEMORABLE CHILDHOOD

One's childhood often surrounded by lot of memories which we used to cherish during our lifetime. These memories are often related to our family and friends. Some of these memories are sweet and some are bitter. If you do have caring and loving parents & grandparents then these memories are always sweet.

The term 'Childhood' itself contains lot of emotions. Our childhood plays a great role in forming our personalities. What we had experienced in our childhood generally formed our behaviour later on. Role of our parents or guardians matters here a lot.

I still remember all the sweet memories attached with my parents & family and only the thoughts of these memories make me feel cheerful. In every situation of my life when I got stuck anywhere or feel distressed, I used to remember those wonderful days which I had left behind and it gives me a wonderful soothing feeling.

I could still feel the touch of my parents, their love & care too. The sensation of those feelings made my mind calm. I feel myself lucky to have the wonderful time in my childhood. We just don't have expensive mobile phones or branded outfits or watches.

As we are 90's kids, our childhood was very simple without all these amenities but still every moment was very beautiful. I never felt need of any gadgets at that time. We used to spend our spare time with our grandparents listening to their life stories, go for an evening walk in nature with them, laugh and play with them. Their unconditional love was just everything for us.

<u>GRANDPA'S LIFE –</u>

My grandparents made childhood of all of us awesome by giving extra affection and care. It's next to impossible to forget the care and love they have provided to us. He had always paid attention to all of our little needs since our childhood to adulthood. I used to share all my stuff whether related to studies or other activities with my grandpa. He always listened to me carefully. I always do enjoy the company of my grandparents a lot.

My grandpa was a family man since always. His top priority was family and then comes the other things. He provided all his kids with utmost care and always inspired them to do excel in studies. Although my grandpa came from a rural background of Haryana and rose without parents by his sister, so he didn't get that much exposure in life. Still, he made the optimum utilisation of every opportunity he got in life and settled down with a government job. He just knew the importance of education and that's why he used to inspire all of us in the family for the same irrespective of whether we will follow him or not.

Grandpa was the one who educated my dad in the best possible manner by sending him to the best school of that time in the town. He used to spend one third of his per month earning on the education of my father. That was really huge amount. But Grandpa wanted him to be successful in life. My father also cracked government job exam and got the job in central railways like my grandfather.

Not only my father, grandpa also helped all four of us grandkids of him in studies. I used to learn reading literature and Shakespeare stories from him. He also helped me in learning various theories of different subjects. I couldn't thank him enough for the contribution made by him in my studies apart from my mother and teachers. He was truly a blessing for me.

My grandpa always had interest in learning. His learning aptitude made him acquire more and more knowledge through teaching all of us. Not only through education but with various other matters, he always kept himself engaged in different activities. The thing I liked the most in him was he always gave ear to me whenever I needed him and give me suggestions that I could follow blindly & trust me the people of my grandpa's age are the best advisors ever because life has already taught them so many lessons.

My grandpa used to share his experiences with all of us. I just love to listen the memories related to his childhood. I remember once he shared about his visit to Allahabad.

There he went to the river Triveni Sangam which is the confluence of the three rivers viz. Ganga, Yamuna, and the mythical Sarasvati River. He didn't know how to swim but he was full of enthusiasm because of his young age so he went near the bank of the river and start going inside slowly. As he stepped forward, the water level rose and reached up to his stomach. He thought to move one more step forward to feel more water so the same he did and his feet got stuck in the sand and he started sinking inside the river. The water level rose and reached up to his chest. He tried very hard to move out of the sand but all his efforts went in vain. Soon the level of water reached up to his chin and with this he almost lost all his hopes to live.

I could only feel that feeling of terror which one could feel in this situation. When suddenly life made you feel like it was your last day to live, all you could think about the deeds you have done so far in life (whether good or bad) and all the dreams which are still unfulfilled. That's why we should always try to live our dreams to the fullest while we are alive. You will never know which day is going to be your last.

Grandpa told me after getting stuck in that situation he thanked God for everything he had so far in life and thought to try for the last time to came out of the sand. He tossed his legs hard in the sand and luckily came out a bit then he started tossing his legs again and again until the water level came down to his chest and slowly came out of the water and somehow managed to save his life.

We all had experienced some kind of difficult or adventurous situations in our life which are impossible to forget. My grandparents used to share with me lot of memories related to their childhood.

My grandma once told me about her childhood. Previously I thought that my grandmom has her origin in India only but that's not the truth. She belongs to Burma country which is now known as Myanmar located in the western portion of mainland Southeast Asia. The British colony of Burma was part of the British run state in India, the Empire of India, from 1824 to 1937. Burma was separated from the rest of the Indian Empire in 1937, just ten years before India became an independent country, in 1947.

After separation many immigrants emerge from Burma to India. My Grandmom was one of them. She came to India with her parents and other family members through water ways and start residing in Haryana state of India. My Grandpa belongs to Rajasthan and was from Marwari Caste who later on shifted to Haryana with family in his early childhood.

So, these were some childhood stories of my grandparents which I used to listen from them. I always cherished to listen to their stories because I never know how much time we had left together. So, I always try to give my 100% to every moment to make them precious. My grandmom used to take me to the market for shopping purpose and sometimes to different temples also to listen to Satsang or ongoing Ramayana path. I could still feel the touch of her soft hands of those childhood time when she used to take me everywhere with her. As my mom was working so my grandmom used to take care of me and my younger sister at home. That's why I'm more attached to my grandparents.

With passage of time, my grand mom got older and she could barely walk alone on roads and found it difficult to cross the road without support. Then I used to take my grand mom for shopping like she used to take me in my childhood. I just love to spend my holidays with her. I used to take her to Satsang and temples too. But no matter how much time I will give her in her old age, I could never repay for all the love and care she had provided to me.

What I Learned –

I got to learn that life's small happiness lies in the moments that we have shared with our loved ones. My grandparents and all other members in my family made my life worth living. I never felt neglected at any moment in my life. I always enjoyed each and every moment.

I could see my childhood like a flashback in front of my eyes. No matter where I am, I could still feel my grandparents and parents sitting in front of me or listening to me or guiding me whenever I needed them. It works like a booster therapy for me whenever I faced any kind of dilemma in my life.

I have learned to make every moment precious and beautiful by putting my 100 % to live that moment in my married life. From 1st day of my marriage, I started enjoying togetherness with my husband. We have travelled together to a lot of places. Even we do have a bucket list to travel to different places all over the world. I never faced any kind of issues in my married life because we both live as friends more than like typical husband wife. We laugh together, share moments together and love to celebrate small moments. We have a lovely daughter too and I give her the same care and affection that I received from my parents and grandparents in my childhood.

It's all because I rose in a perfect manner by my parents that's why I'm able to pass on the same to the next generation of mine. One's childhood matters a lot in deciding our future as well as future of our kids. Just remember the good memories and learn from the bad ones, that's the secret to live a happy life.

CHAPTER EIGHT

SCHOOL DAYS

Twinkle Twinkle little star, How I wonder what you are......!!!!! A very common rhyme we all taught at school which we could still remember.

School days were awesome right!!

The term school made us remember lot of memories related to our friends and teachers etc. School time comprised of very long journey of our life which we share with our friends and teachers. It's the time when we gain the knowledge of the world around us as well as learn to socialize with others. We learn the way of living and way to tackle different situations in life through different experiences during school life. Overall school plays a great role in forming our nature.

School time becomes much fun when you do have loveable grandparents who do loves you daily after you get back to home from school. You feel so much pampered in their company. Lucky are those who got both of them.

GRANDPA'S LIFE –

My grandpa used to share his school days memories with me. I remember he termed his teachers as 'Master ji' which is quite common during those days of newly independent India. During those times education used to be given in government schools. Slowly with passage of time privatisation took place and education becomes the business. Our grandparents belong to those government schools where discipline is being taught by the teachers at initial stage.

I remember I used to return from my school with my grandfather. My mother was the teacher in that same school. She is still teaching there. I used to go to the school with my mom but used to come back with my grandpa. He used to wait for me at the same place near the stage of our school. Even my friends could see him from the distance. My friends also admire my grandpa a lot.

He came for me on daily basis whether it was hot or cold or even rainy season. I could never forget all those seasons. I used to enjoy the rain also while coming back to home. Grandpa used to carry my bag and bottle and listen to my daily activities at school. I used to share every little detail of my every day with him. On the way he used to ask me what my teacher has taught.

My grandpa was a part-time accountant at a business of kiln. He used to take me to his workplace while returning home from school. I used to cherish his company a lot. There I used to sit for some time until my grandpa finished his work. Then after coming home my grandmom used to take care of me. We used to watch movies of the old Bollywood cinema together until my mom came back from school.

Ah! What the golden days those were.

What I Learned -

Apart from my mother my grandpa was the one who taught me in the evening time, I used to have a routine to take my books to him for the purpose of study. Although I know all the things, he was teaching to me in advance due to my school and mom but still I like to revise all the same with my grandpa on daily basis. It used to give me the inner satisfaction spending time with my grandparents. My grandpa also was very conscious for my studies. He wanted me to be the successful one in my career. He used to admire whenever I got first rank in my class. Also, he used to share the same news with his friend circle. All these little moments gave me the happiness for the lifetime.

Sometimes I wonder now that how much time I really got to spend with him because the year I born he got retired from his services. Now at this age I came to know the real meaning of retirement at sixty. Retirement at sixty means you gave all your life doing any service and now your age is not allowing you more to do the same. It means that you are now free to rest from all of your responsibilities and now the time comes to spend with your children and grandchildren. I feel myself lucky that I have spent nearly 26 years of my life with my grandpa. That's really huge in itself. That's why I am still so much attached with my both grandparents.

They have taught me to live in the family and the value of family as well. Regardless of everything that you achieve in this material world none can replace the family. Family the word itself do have the power to channelise your energy in the right direction. You can win the world if you do have a family. It works like the support system one need in our difficult times.

CHAPTER NINE

SILENT CRY

"Death is not the greatest loss in life. The greatest loss in life is what dies inside us while we are still alive."

There is time in everyone's life when he/she thought that his/her life is a total mess. At some point of time in our lives we do face anxiety, depression or suicidal thoughts. Sometimes it appears that life is not that much worthy to live. When we are unable to fulfil any goal then life appears meaningless to us or if we are unable to set a goal then also, we feel distress.

Sometimes we do miss some old memories with our special one's and knew well that we are unable to recreate them or unable to bring back those persons in our lives again because either that person doesn't exist anymore or not in our contact at present.

Sometimes we just thought that life is running so fast and we are unable to catch or most preferably I want to use 'live' ..., Yes, it's true that we are unable to live every moment. Life is just running like wind and we are running like clouds. Some clouds know where to rain and get in touch with the life again and some just wipe away with air and lost forever.

We all do feel heavy at some point of time in our lives. This heaviness becomes difficult to tackle when we don't know how to handle the same. In such situations it's better to cry out aloud like no one is listening. Cry your heart out to reduce such heaviness and only then you could see the life as it is.

It's necessary to reduce the burden of your thoughts to see the reality of life.

Life is not something that we are living or thinking we are spending well. Sit for a moment and look back at your past to see how far you have come and how many memories you have created. Now just remember the good memories only and forget the bad ones and start living in present to create some good memories again to cherish in future. Your present is going to be your past after just a second and you are creating your future by living in NOW.

<u>GRANDPA'S LIFE –</u>

I have never seen my grandpa feeling down. He was very strong since his childhood. I have only seen contentment and peacefulness in his nature. And yes, it's true, He was truly a gem in our family. My grandpa spends his life with discipline. His nature was always cheerful with all of us grandkids and used to motivate us to do better in exams and in every phase of life.

In June 2017, when my grandpa got fracture in his hip bone, he became unable to walk for few days. He has got his operation done after 2-3 days of injury with the best doctor of our area. Doctor suggested physiotherapy to my grandpa to be able to walk again. And he gave his life one more chance to flourish again. He learned to walk with the help of physiotherapy and with help of all of us family members. Initially he had lost all his hope to stand up again on his feet but gradually with time he took it as a challenge in that age and able to walk again. I could feel all that learning was like an infant learning to walk from crawling stage.

In all those moments I felt my grandpa was crying silently and only the attached ones could feel the same.

<u>*What I Learned -*</u>

Every kid does have a different kind of attachment with his/her grandparents but the first-born grandkid does have the more among all. I could personally feel the same. All my siblings don't have that connection with grandparents as I do have. I was so much attached with them that even today I could feel that sensitiveness inside me for them. I can't explain my love and emotions for them in words. They were like whole world for me with whom I never want to get separated. I do enjoy their company from the bottom of my heart because somewhere I know that it won't last forever. That's why I did value all those moments that I was spending with them.

I really can't see them sad in any single moment. May be as a kid I won't be able to understand what troubles they were going through at that time. I have only seen the happy faces of them. So, the day when I saw my grandpa crying out of pain and that hopelessness in his eyes, that day was the worst day of my life. I never wanted him to face any kind of pain. But I also was unable to control the situations of his life too. This made me feel that no matter how much you do love someone, if something is meant to happen in their life you just can't control the same. One need to deal with their physical and mental pain all by themselves only.

CHAPTER TEN

LAST DAY OUT

In life there are many things we didn't realize that we are doing for the last time. When we meet someone in our life, greet him in such a gentle way so as to leave an impression on his/her mind forever because there are certain persons may be with whom we are meeting for the last time.

Time do passes away, but touching words by someone remain in our memories forever. Our image could leave an unforgettable impression in someone's mind.

When we do visit some places to explore then make the most out of your trip because in your lifetime maybe you won't get another chance to visit there again. In short just try to give your best shot in every moment of your life because life won't happen again, if passed away. And we could never know which day is our last day out.

GRANDPA'S LIFE –

It's 10th October, 2018, my grandpa's condition is getting worse because he was not eating anything for past few days. Therefore, I and my Cha-cha decided to take him to the doctor in the ambulance. We called the ambulance and took him to the doctor. We didn't know at that time that it's the last trip outside for my grandpa.

In the way, grandpa was looking outside lying on the stretcher of the ambulance.

He said to me- "I have seen this city growing before my eyes. A few years back there were not many facilities here. The education was very expensive. I used to spend one third of my earnings on the education of your dad and rest to manage whole family. I prefer to walk everywhere rather to use any means of transport. There were many trees around the city at that time and less pollution. Environment was enriched of flora and fauna. Rest the city wasn't that much populated as it seems now. Now I can't walk freely here. I used to get scared from the fast-moving vehicles and busy roads. Everything is changed now"

Then we stopped at the hospital. Doctor took almost half an hour to visit to my grandpa. Meanwhile my grandpa got emotional and said – "I have seen this hospital developing before me. There was nothing when I came to the Modi Nagar at an early age of 11 years. These all doctors were new and young at that time. I used to visit here for a walk with my friends."

He was missing all the good memories associated with his past life. We all do the same at some point of time in our lives. But for mesmerizing the same we need to create some with our loved ones.

Then the doctor arrived. My grandpa had severe stomach pain for past few days due to intensifying cancer cells. Doctor checked him, prescribed him some more medicines and told us that grandpa won't survive for long now because cancer cells had started multiplying themselves and affecting other organs of the body like liver and lungs. These cancer cells will get burst one day by themselves and that day would probably be his last day. Doctor didn't give us any false hope.

That's the reason my grandpa had lost his appetite. He didn't eat anything well for past 15 days almost. I didn't know how he was handling all such pain without any complaints. He never said to us to take him to the doctor. He never did demand of anything. Even today I can't imagine how someone could possess that much patience. He was the true definition of patience for me.

What I learned –

That day I got the real meaning of the name of my grandpa -
"SAHAJ RAM GUPTA"

Yeah, that's what his name is. The person in whose name the simplicity itself exists, imagine how much could it be there in his nature. He was a simple person with no desires of having luxurious life. If he wanted, he could live his life in more comfort. But he chooses to remain ambitionless but enthusiastic towards life.

He neither did have interest in new garments nor he wanted to taste street food. He lived a simple life being a complete family man. He didn't have a cunning mind either. I have never seen someone with so much of qualities in my life.

He just never groaned even if he was in so much of pain and that was the part of his nature. He just wanted to live more but life didn't bless him with the same.

So, I think we should really be grateful for all the blessings and good things that life has provided to us because life could snatch it all at once without asking for our permission. There are things on which we don't have any control and death is one of among those.

Be expressive in every moment because tomorrow may not come. Laugh as much as you can if you are laughing. Cry as much as you can if you are crying. Feel joyful as much as you can if you are on outing. Just be expressive and live your life for yourself. If you could learn to live for yourself only then you could learn to live for others

CHAPTER ELEVEN

THE ESCHATON

There is a quote – "When you were born you were crying and everybody else was smiling. Live your life in such a way, so at the end you're the one who is smiling and everyone else is crying."

I just love this saying but rare could live their life in such a way. It's the biggest pleasure to know that people around you love you and do care for you. It shows that the way you have lived your life created some impact on the mind of others. It means that we have left some impression on their mind for ever. Not all manage to do the same. You really need a charismatic personality for being the same.

Death is a word beyond which our mind can't think. It's something where our imagination ends. It means the end of everything for us. After death nothing really matters i.e., the wealth or money issues, health related issues, family issues etc. These all problems exist when we are alive only. And in the end if you have to go leaving everything behind then what's the point of taking so much tensions in life. Why we all can't live our life in a peaceful manner??

Why to think that we should escape doing this or that because of what others will think or react on the same??

What others will think that's their problem. We just can't change everybody's perception for us.

Take rest for one minute and take a deep breath and think like there is no one who is watching you. You are all alone in this world. There is no one to interfere with your decisions. It's your life and you are the commander. Feel this freedom. There is no one to bound you for feeling this way. Now just feel the immense pleasure.

Yeah, it's true that you are bound by society, culture, family, responsibilities in the outside materialistic world but inside you are free to think anything. We should try to give our life some meaning with the help of this freedom. Otherwise, time is just passing and our whole life will pass in a blink.

Just start doing that much awaited task that you always wanted to do. Even if you can't give your whole time to that work due to busy schedule. Give at least 10 minutes to yourself in doing that thing which you really love and continue this practise on daily basis. You will notice that change will start to happen not rapidly but slowly. Those 10 minutes a day could change your life forever only if you start following your passion.

I personally feel that we always face a failure due to lack of consistency. There is nothing in this world which we can't achieve if we are consistent and determined enough to get the same. Ultimately, we all have to go from this world sooner or later. Nobody knows when and how. At least do something that will create an impact on your life as well as life of others. First, we'll need to get up for ourselves only then something could be done for the welfare of the society.

If we introspect ourselves, we will realise that we have left a meaningless life behind and NOW is the time to add some meaning to it. So that we could really rest in peace at the end.

Grandpa's life –

One more morning of 20th October 2018 and my grandpa was still struggling from cancer. A few days before his stomach got thick and it's looking like there were some tumours of cancer formed inside which were extreme painful beyond our imagination. He was in extreme pain due to the swollen tummy. Grandpa also want to get rid of the same that's why he was starving himself for almost last 30 days or maybe it was due to the cancer. He didn't eat anything. Doctor kept him on drip of glucose and medicines in our home under care of a medical staff.

Grandpa even stop sharing his needs with us. He neither asks us for food or anything. Only one thing he do ask is for water. We gave him water with the help of spoon by opening his mouth by ourselves. He became this much weak that he was even unable to open his mouth.

He always said to me that he wanted a simple death where someone slept overnight and never opened his eyes all over again but destiny didn't give him this opportunity. He never wanted to have such a painful death but no one knows how they are going to die.

On that particular morning of 20th October his swollen tummy suddenly looks like flat one. It was like tumours got burst inside his tummy. He was groaning in pain. As it was the fourth stage of cancer so doctors didn't have any cure for him. We could do nothing for him except watching and that was the most painful situation for all of us.

At that time even I did have the thought that it's better to die than to bear such pain. Nobody else could feel your physical pain only they could console you and pray to God to bless you with strength to bear such pain. There is no point of living such a helpless and painful life knowing that you can't get back to normal again due to age pressure.

Thinking in the same way for that person whom you admire the most and without whom you can't live with ease is so difficult.

Then it's 10 AM in the morning.

We all were at home except my mother. She went for her job that day. Grandpa suddenly start groaning in pain. We all gathered in his room. I can't ever forget that scene when my grandmom was there holding the hands of my grandpa and had tears in her eyes. My father was giving spoonful of water again and again to my grandpa but that was of no use. He was groaning continuously. Then my father called the doctor and told him the situation of my grandpa and requested him to visit our home as soon as possible.

We all were in tears and praying to God for their wellbeing. I was reading 18th chapter of our holy Bhagwat Geeta and as soon as

I finished the same. I realised that my grandpa has closed his eyes.

I screamed "Baba, please do open your eyes."

Suddenly my whole childhood flashed back before my eyes. That was the same bed where my grandpa used to teach me various subjects in my school time.

That was the same room where I spend my whole childhood listening to my grandpa's jokes and various talks.

That was the same room where I used to see my grandparents together.

That was the same room where I used to see him reading scriptures and doing his accounting work.

That was the same room that's not going to remain same again at least for me after that day.

That moment was like someone has snatched the soul of that room and not of my grandpa's body.

Then at 10.30 AM –

My grandpa took his last deep breath with closed eyes.

And everything got finished in a moment.

He was no more.

I don't have the words to describe the pain that I was feeling on that particular day.

Everything got stopped for a second.

I hold the hands of my grandpa. I could feel that sensation even today. The soft touch but lifeless hands. I touched grandpa's grey hairs and tried to make him open his eyes again but every effort was in vain.

My father was talking to doctor at that moment. I called him and said that my grandpa was not moving. His heart stopped beating. Blood circulation in veins got stopped.

And yeah, that was the moment I saw someone passed away right before my eyes and that someone was my grandpa.

.

.

.

.

.

.

I wish I could make everything good again.

.

.

I wish my grandpa could live for some more years.

.

.

I was unable to gather the courage to look at my grandmom at that time.

66.5 years of togetherness suddenly came to an end.

My grandmom was in deep shock. She was saying again and again – "I am unable to accept this fact that you are not anymore"

"Why you left me alone here?"

"What I will do without you?"

"I wanted to die before you."

I have never seen someone sobbing continuously for 6 hours until all took away the dead body of my grandpa from home to cemetery. She cried her heart out that day.

My father called the doctor after my grandpa took his last breath. Doctor confirmed all of us that our grandpa is no more. Then I informed my mom and my father informed all the other relatives.

All the rituals were performed. I touched my grandpa's feet for the last time to take his blessings. And grandpa was taken away from that home forever.

I don't want to remember that day again in my life.

We all left alone in that lifeless home to spend the rest of our lives.

.

.

.

.

I didn't want to enter in my grandpa's room in that evening.

I wanted him to attend my wedding ceremony in December which has become quite impossible for everyone to enjoy.

But time doesn't stop for anyone.

Slowly everyone came out of shock with passage of time and started to behave normally again. We try to keep our grandmom engage here and there all the time so that she could gather strength to bear such huge loss.

Life started moving on again.

Epilogue

Every ending comes with a new beginning. I got to realise this when I lost my grandpa. He was the person who is unforgettable to me. Living life without him from the very next morning looks like meaningless. Everyone in home was missing him badly. The things grandpa leftover behind him reminding us of his presence in the home. The holy scriptures he used to read, his pocket radio, his watch which he was using since 90's, his stick for walking purpose after the operation, his accounting work, his plants etc. made us feel restless again and again.

The hardest part is to watch grandmom sitting alone in the grandpa's room. She used to miss her daily talks with grandpa. They both do spend the quality time together. Grandmom always makes the tea in the evening for grandpa and she continued this practice even after his demise. Grandmom made the tea daily and put it before grandpa's photo frame. Seeing her daily like this make me feel quiver and sorrowful.

I used to feel pity for my grandmom and thought what was the fault of her and why was she feeling this pain. But time gradually made me realise that this is the harsh reality of life. You need to accept the truth and continue with the same.

We need to find ways of happiness for ourselves. You need to divert your mind in the things which you always wanted to do. Thinking about the same things all over again will surely bring unhappiness in your life. You need to get over from your current situation and only you yourself could do that for you not anyone else. Others could only listen to your thoughts and could console you but you need to get up for yourself.

Do cry out loud whenever you wanted to cry. Don't stop yourself from not crying. Crying won't make you weak but stronger. With every tear shed from your eyes all the resentment also vanishes.

It's not the end when someone moves away from your life. We don't realise the same but somewhere we become dependent on the other person for living happily and we thought life can't be possible without him. But that's not true, in fact it's the beginning of the new life without that person. Now it's time to learn to live without that special one. Do miss that special partner of you at times but don't act like everything is lost.

Life doesn't wait. You need to continue with the same or either you could spend the rest in crying forever.

I kept my grandpa alive in my memories even today. I do remember him in all the ups and downs of my life. I do remember his teachings. I do remember the ways he had lived his life. I do remember the happy time which I had spent with him and which made my childhood extra special. He didn't go anywhere for me. He has always been there in my heart. I used to see my grandpa in my dreams and discuss all my troubles with him and got the good advice too. He became the voice of my heart now that I could listen anytime anywhere no matter what.